# Beginning with me

## Meditations with a challenge

ST PAULS

Cover design by courtesy of San Pablo (Ediciones Paulinas) Argentina

ST PAULS
Middlegreen, Slough SL3 6BT, United Kingdom
Moyglare Road, Maynooth, Co. Kildare, Ireland

© Anthea Dove 1996
ISBN 085439 518 0
Set by TuKan, High Wycombe
Printed by Redwood Books, Trowbridge

ST PAULS is an activity of the priests and brothers of the
Society of St Paul who proclaim the Gospel through the media
of social communication

# BEGINNING WITH ME

*This book is dedicated to*
*Nadir Dinshaw and Anthony Gittins*
*in appreciation of who they are and what they do*

# Contents

# Foreword

This is a book of meditations which can be used daily during Lent or at any other time. In spite of its title, the book is not really about me, except in so far as it is a sharing of some of the insights I have been given over the years.

I am getting old now. Being old does not necessarily mean being wise, but it does mean that we have had a chance to look at things in different lights, perhaps sometimes to see beyond the obvious or to find new meanings in happenings and situations.

Each meditation in the book has three parts: a story, a prayer and a reflection on the story. Some readers may decide to omit the prayer and the reflection, preferring to respond to the meditation in their own way.

Although in some cases I have changed names and unimportant details, to save embarrassment for the people concerned, all the stories in this book are essentially true. The majority of them are concerned with some aspect of justice or injustice.

It seems to me that what is asked of us as Christians, above all, is that we should love one another. And if we love one another we have no choice but to seek justice, both in the world outside and far away, and in the small exchanges of everyday life.

# Beginning with me

Bishop John Crowley who has travelled to developing countries in different parts of the world as part of his work with CAFOD, the Catholic Fund for Overseas Development, was in Southern Ethiopia when the famine was at its height. He watched a queue of small children lining up to receive their meagre ration of food from Aid workers. He was told that food was so short that it could only be given to children under four.

Some of the little ones were too small or too weak to feed themselves, and so their older brothers and sisters, for whom there was nothing to eat, patiently fed them without taking a morsel for themselves.

The story stunned me. I wondered how young children, themselves desperately hungry, could behave with such restraint and, above all, selflessness. The children belonged to a country far from mine. Their skins were a different colour. They were probably un-educated. I do not know if they believed in God.

I spent a little while thinking about these children, trying to imagine what they were like, and all the time wondering about their unselfish love. Then I began to think about the people I live among. Ours is a society far wealthier, far better educated, much more sophisti-cated. We are strong; by the world's standards, success-ful. The Ethiopian refugees were the "anawim", the

11

dispossessed, among the weakest people on earth. Some of us believe in God, and some of us find the idea of selflessness ludicrous. "Number One First" is sadly all too often the motto which not only individuals but even nations seem happy to live by.

I felt sad when I thought about all this, but after I switched on the radio and listened to one of our leading politicians talking about our membership of the European community, I felt a great deal of impotent anger. The minister was obviously trying to please the British voters, and talking about his hopes for what we can get out of Europe. He said nothing about what we might give to Europe, or what we might learn from the other countries who are our neighbours.

The night after I had heard this minister's speech, I set off for a prayer meeting which I attend every Monday. I was preoccupied as I walked along the road to the church hall, thinking again with admiration of the Ethiopian children, so generous and so brave, thinking with dismay about the prevailing attitude of selfishness in my own country, thinking with indignation of those leaders who feed their ambition by pandering to our self-interest, and who encourage us to be "out for what we can get".

In spite of these reflections I must have been walking quite fast because I arrived early at the church hall. I went into the little room where we hold our meetings. There was no-one else there yet and I was glad. It meant that I could stake my claim to the most comfortable chair and move it nearer the fire...

Midway across the room I hesitated. Someone, something ... could it have been my guardian angel? Or even the Holy Spirit? ... stopped me in my tracks and managed to get through to me. In that moment I realised a humbling truth.

Selflessness, like peace, like justice, like courage, like generosity, has to begin with me.

*Dear Lord, I see that I blunder foolishly and insensitively through life, so quick to criticise others, so self-righteous in my judgement of them.*

*You said, "Why do you observe the splinter in your brother's eye and never notice the plank in your own?" (Mt 7:3 JB).*

*Help me to see more clearly, to understand the workings of my own mind and heart.*

*Give me the openness and the courage to make a fresh start. "Renew a right spirit within me" (Ps 51:10 AV).*

# Dermot

I was very sad when Dermot died. He was only about forty years old, gentle, humorous, intuitive, self-effacing.

In the daytime he had some sort of humdrum office job, and most evenings he worked among the street people of Soho. Sometimes, when he had a free evening, he would sing for us, and it was a pleasure to listen to his plaintive Irish songs.

I went to his funeral. I thought I was in good time but the huge church was full and I had to stand at the back. By standing on tiptoe I could just see the coffin. Since there were so many mourners I would have expected it to be heaped with flowers, but there was just a single bunch of red roses.

I was curious. I whispered to Jim, a friend who had known Dermot much better than I did, "Whose flowers would those be?" He answered without hesitation. "I expect they're from Shirley?" Then the service began and I couldn't ask who Shirley was.

But at the end, as the chief mourners processed down the aisle, Jim whispered, "That's Shirley." He indicated a beautiful young woman who was walking close behind the coffin with tears streaming down her face.

"She was a prostitute," Jim said, "one of so many

Dermot befriended and helped. She's got a good job now. She thought the world of him."

Afterwards, as I came down the steps outside the church, a passer-by, seeing the great crowd of people issuing from the building, said

"Was it somebody important?"

I didn't hesitate. "YES!" I said.

\*\*\*\*\*

*Lord, I thank you for the life of Dermot who touched the lives of so many others by his love.*

\*\*\*\*\*

This morning, at the back of my church, I saw a poster advertising three days of prayer for the canonisation of John Henry Newman. I admire Newman very much; I think he was a man of outstanding holiness and intelligence. It is impossible to know how many thousands of people have benefited from his wisdom.

And yet, if I were to give up three days for prayer, I would rather pray for those people Dermot worked among, and those like them who walk the streets of our cities. They were – at least in the eyes of most people – sinners, and he ate and drank with them. Lives were transformed by his love.

No-one would dream of proposing Dermot's canonisation, but in his quiet, compassionate way he too was a saint.

# Stranger

Living in Britain, we are very conscious of the evil of racism. Asians, West Indians, Africans and others are too often not only discriminated against but brutally attacked, simply because they belong to an "alien" race.

Because I am white and English through and through, because I and all my ancestors were born here, I am unlikely to be a victim of racism in this country.

But once the boot was on the other foot. I was a stranger, an alien, an outsider, a white woman living among the Malayali people of South India. I might have been a victim of racism. But let me tell you a true story.

With my husband I was invited to a party to celebrate a Muslim wedding. I was new in the country and quite ignorant of the local manners and customs. I was going to a party, so I put on my most beautiful dress. It was flame-coloured, with a full skirt and as was the fashion at that time it had a low-cut bodice which left my shoulders and arms completely bare.

When we arrived at the house, to my surprise the father of the bride straightaway took my husband off. A small figure, dressed in a lovely black sari, approached me. I guessed (I am still guessing!) that it was the bride's mother. All I could see of her were her dark eyes and fine nose and mouth.

We made the traditional greeting (Namasthe!) and then she beckoned me to follow her into a room, where I found about fifteen more small women attired in the same manner. They were sitting in a circle, cross-legged on the floor, and when I came in, feeling by this time unbearably foolish, they greeted me with warm bright smiles. Clumsily, I joined the circle and tried to sit with my legs crossed. By English standards I am only a medium-sized woman, but in that circle I felt huge and awkward and almost naked. My expanse of bare white flesh seemed singularly unattractive.

I knew no words yet of Malayalam and they had no English. We managed to communicate a little by means of signs, and although we sat like this for over an hour, all the women continued to smile.

I was very relieved when a servant came in and I realized that we were going to share a meal. But nobody moved, and the boy came round with banana leaves which he gave to us to place on the floor in front of each of us. Then another man came in with a huge pot and a ladle. He carefully served us each a portion of wonderful-smelling biriani, straight onto the leaf. I waited for my knife and fork until I saw that all the other women had begun to eat, with their fingers. They ate with delicacy; not one of them spilt a drop.

That biriani tasted every bit as good as its smell had promised, but alas, much of it landed on my lap, on the skirt of my beautiful flame-coloured dress, and on the floor.

My new friends did not look at me with disapproval, nor did they stare. If I caught anyone's eye, invariably that eye was smiling. The Muslim women were courteous and gracious to the last, and although it was a great relief when we finally went home, I was a little sad, too, to leave that band of welcoming, accepting people.

I was a stranger and they gave me welcome.

*****

*Lord, help me to welcome as my sisters and brothers all who seem alien in any way: those of different race, religion or background to mine. Let me be willing to learn from those whose ways are not my ways, and always to remember that you have no favourites; that all of us are equal in your sight.*

*****

I know about racism at first hand, because I have an adopted West Indian son. When he came to us at the age of three, small white children of his own age accepted him without question and played happily with him.

But a few years later, everything changed. Older children mocked and jeered, making ape-like gestures and calling him "Jungle Bunny". He is a grown man now, and the other day he came home with a blood-soaked bandage across his forehead. He had been quietly sitting in a park when two white youths rushed across and one broke a bottle on his head.

Much worse incidents than this occur every day in our country, and so when I remember how I was treated by black people in their land, I am humbled and saddened.

We are so proud of our British sportsmen, like Linford Christie and Devon Malcolm, we enjoy being entertained by Lennie Henry or Andy Peters, and yet the majority of black people in our country are treated with condescension, or contempt, or outright cruelty.

It seems that the cause of most racism is fear, fear of the unfamiliar, fear of losing employment or the value of property. And if not fear, then ignorance. It is especially sad when children learn to be racist from their parents. Education – through our schools and the media and our churches, seems to be the only answer.

# The end of the party

Ann's life had been a long struggle. Her parents had died when she was very young and although the man she married, Joe, was gentle and considerate, he became a long-term depressive after he had been unemployed for several years.

But Ann was a noticeably happy person. Her only child, Sarah, gave her great joy. She was a bright-faced girl, affectionate, and vivacious. To her parents' surprise and wonder, she was also highly intelligent and had qualified as a barrister.

Ann was very careful with the little money she had, and from one year to the next she saved up for Sarah's birthday parties. Ever since she was a small girl, on the 21st March every year, there was a celebration at Ann's house for all Sarah's friends. Of course as she grew older the friends changed and the kind of party changed too. This year Sarah would be twenty-five and Ann was determined it would be the best yet. She even got Joe to decorate the whole house.

Everything went well, even better than Ann had dared to hope. The food was very much appreciated; the young people's faces were flushed with wine and laughter. After the meal Sarah played her guitar and the house was filled with singing.

Much later, when everyone had said goodnight and those who were sleeping in the house had gone to bed, Sarah came downstairs and found Ann finishing off the washing up.

"Mum!" she exclaimed "you promised to leave it till the morning... you know, you're hopeless!" She put her arms round Ann and gave her a big hug. Then she said "You're so good to me!"

Her voice broke a little. She sounded almost tearful. That wasn't like Sarah. Ann looked closely at her and said, "Sarah, is something the matter?"

Sarah tried to keep her voice steady. "Yes, Mum. I'm sorry – I had a test for HIV and the result came through yesterday. It's positive."

*****

*Dear Lord, we know that you are close to the broken-hearted. But not everyone is aware of your presence at the heart of their suffering.*

*May no-one have to endure intense grief and pain entirely alone. And may all people with AIDS be supported in love.*

*****

I think it is impossible for those of us who are not HIV positive or do not have AIDS even to imagine what it must be like. Not only is it a very frightening and painful disease in itself, but those who contract it are so often stigmatized, avoided, rejected as outcasts even by their own families. In addition to their pain, people with AIDS sometimes suffer from extreme loneliness.

There is a striking parallel with the way lepers used to be treated. Sadly the same people who are horrified at the callousness of the Jews in the days of Jesus are sometimes the ones who judge and condemn people with AIDS. Even some Christians have declared their belief that AIDS is a punishment from God.

This disease is a cruel scourge which affects saints as well as sinners, and people with AIDS deserve all our understanding and compassion.

# Holiness

The old priest spoke quietly. He held his audience as much by his sincerity and conviction as by what he was saying. He was talking about prayer, and how essential it is if we are to become open and receptive and sensitive to life and creation.

Then he surprised us by telling a story against himself. He told us how he got up early the other morning and went into his church to pray. He knelt, silent and attentive, listening to God.

Suddenly the peaceful silence was shattered. A parishioner burst into the church, clattered up the aisle to where the priest was kneeling and began to make noisy demands.

The old man's precious moments of communion with God had been blasted away. Violent anger erupted as he turned to face the intruder and shouted, "Get out!"

Seconds later he was overcome by remorse. He had turned away someone who had come to him as the Word of God.

*****

*Dear Lord, I thank you for this holy and honest old man. Help us to grow in self-knowledge and integrity, so that we may be at one with you and with all your children.*

*****

It seems hard that however much and however sincerely we try to become holy, most of us never quite manage it. God has a disconcerting habit of pulling us up short.

The old priest who told this story was a good man, humble, honest, faithful and loving towards God and all those who served in his parish. He strove to be more like God, to come closer to God, to deepen his prayer life. Surely nothing could be more commendable, more right. And yet... and yet in the very middle of his prayerful contemplation, he lost his self-control and vented unreasonable anger on an innocent if thoughtless parishioner.

From this incident, he learnt of his own frailty and weakness, of how he had still to go far in the pursuit of holiness. And we, who read this story, aware that he told it of himself, perhaps wish that we were as near to God as he already is.

# Cheerful giver

A Parsee friend of mine told me about his grand-mother who lived in Karachi. She was gentle and gracious, loved by everyone. She was also generous to a fault, and her family were well aware of that fault.

"Granny" was giving away her possessions: jewel-lery and clothes, at an alarming rate, so something had to be done. Her daughters took the bold step of lock-ing away her saris and taking the key.

Soon afterwards, when the daughters were out, a poor woman came to the house and begged for some-thing to wear. The old lady was distressed and apolo-getic.

"I am so sorry" she said, "but I cannot let you have anything. You see, my childen have locked all my clothes away and they have gone out with the key."

The poor woman was looking at the sari my friend's grandmother was wearing.

"Your sari is very beautiful" she said.

Straightaway the grandmother took off her sari and gave it to the woman. When the daughters came home they were not pleased to find their mother sitting in her petticoat.

"But what could I do?" she asked them humbly, with her innocent logic. "The poor woman wanted it so I gave it to her."

*****

*Dear Lord, I thank you for all the holy men and women who lead hidden lives of goodness. I thank you for those who keep their innocence throughout their lives, and for those whose generosity is an inspiration.*

*****

We are told that God loves a cheerful giver (cf. 2 Cor 9:7) and some people are wonderfully generous with their money, their possessions, their time and their concern.

Today in our society there is a shocking emphasis on the importance of money. For many who have no creed to provide them with different values, the chief goal in life is the acquisition of wealth, and with it, in some cases, power. In our hospitals and schools, everything has to be cost-effective, sometimes to the detriment of patients and pupils.

Such policies foster greed, and greed is the opposite of generosity. Where people have not been given faith in God, or learnt to value truth and goodness, they learn instead to worship other gods, like wealth and power, and to live by other values, grabbing rather than giving.

But in every society, throughout the ages, I believe there will be cheerful givers like the woman in the gospel who gave two mites to the temple treasury (cf. Mk 12:42) and the Parsee grandmother who gave away her sari.

# Brian's story

Brian is a bereavement counsellor. Here is his story.

"This must be the last time," I said firmly to myself as I trudged up the long mile to Donna's house.

As well as feeling tired and frustrated because it seemed a futile waste of my time, I was conscious that I was not doing a good job as a bereavement counsellor.

Admittedly Donna talked non-stop for an hour and I did my best to listen attentively to every word, but somehow we had got way off track – bereavement didn't figure in the session any more.

So I was definitely resolved to tell Donna that this would be the last time. She opened the door to me, unresponsive to my smile as usual, and to my surprise said, "I do appreciate you coming."

I was thrown by this statement, not only because it was the first time Donna had made any mention that my visits were helpful to her, but because the word "appreciate" must have cost her something to say. Donna's vocabulary is basic and almost exclusively monosyllabic.

As with most people my confidence soars at the merest hint of praise. Maybe I wasn't such a failure after all. More importantly, I realised that for some inexplicable reason Donna needed me or thought she needed me. Before I had sat down, I had changed my mind. I would go on visiting her.

As I listened to Donna, I understood that all the things she had previously told me, even including her sister's death, were only surface problems. This morning she chose – or perhaps found the courage – to reveal what her life was really like.

I sat there, holding all those counselling techniques: body language, eye contact etc. in the back of my mind, experiencing shock and horror, wondering how much of this to show, aware that my eyes were literally stretching wider and wider. I hoped I was making the appropriate noises.

And all the while I was silently saying "O my God!" over and over, praying for Donna, praying for myself that I might be of some use to her.

Some of my friends criticise me for watching "Eastenders". "Real life isn't like that" they say. Real life is much worse for Donna.

She came to a pause in her narrative and said, "There is nobody who knows what it's like. I don't know nobody who has been through it like me."

For a crazy second I found myself wishing I was a single parent living in inadequate housing, hooked on tranquillisers, in constant physical pain, regularly battered and raped. Then I could have said to Donna: "I know."

But of course I don't know, thank God. Like the vast majority of counsellors I am middle-class and well educated. I have experienced different kinds of suffering, but I have never had to live in real poverty and in fear of my life, in a situation where being in debt and unloved seem only peripheral. That is outside my experience and my imagining.

And where is God in all this? I have no doubt that

he is loving Donna and suffering with her, but I am not going to talk to her about him, not yet. To do so would be like preaching to a starving child before giving him bread.

All that I can do is listen and pray and go on visiting Donna.

*****

*Lord, let us not lose courage. Help us to show our love by listening to others with attention and respect.*

*****

Perhaps it is always impossible to stand in someone else's shoes. Sometimes we cannot even begin to imagine what it is like to be in another person's situation. The very rich have little idea how it is to be poor, and vice versa. The happily married cannot know what it means to be divorced or a struggling single parent. Those who suffer constant pain can only wonder how it feels to be in perfect health.

That is why organisations such as Alcoholics Anonymous and Gamblers Anonymous and the many others who cater for people who are "in the same boat" are so successful.

But there are occasions when people in very different boats find themselves together, where one person is in need and the other trying to help. There is no point, then, in pretending to understand, to know what it is like. All we can do is stand or sit alongside and listen with full attention and genuine concern for the one who is in need.

# Resurrection

Theologians and scholars argue about the Resurrection. Did Jesus really rise bodily from the grave? Or is it that his Spirit is alive and with us for ever?

There can be few Christians who do not at some time or other suffer from doubt, about this or about the very existence of God.

Once at a time when my own faith was a bit shaky, some friends from London came to stay with us. They arrived late on a Friday after a long journey, and Prue came in behind a big bouquet of Spring flowers which she had carried all the way. It was the dead end of winter, the greyest, dullest time of the year, and the beautiful irises and narcissi were like a sunburst.

We were delighted with the flowers but even more to see Prue and John after a long separation. A lot happened at once: the hugs and greetings, showing them their room, putting supper on the table, putting the flowers in a vase.

We had a very pleasant evening and slept well. In the morning I got up first and went downstairs. There on the table stood my vase, and everyone of the lovely Spring flowers looked dead. They were not just drooping; their stems were completely bent over and their heads lay on the table. Shocked and dismayed I picked up the vase. It was empty. In my excitement the night before I had failed to put any water in it.

My husband quickly filled it to the brim with water but I felt it was an empty gesture. I went out to get some bread and when I returned the irises and narcissi were standing up, fresh and healthy, and beautiful as before, risen from the dead.

I stared at them, filled with wonder and joy.

Like everyone in our sad world, I am used to seeing pictures of dying children on our screens, and homeless people curled up on doorsteps. What can a few flowers, living or dead, matter in the scheme of things?

And yet for me that tiny incident meant a resurgence of hope and a confirmation of faith. The flowers were alive; Jesus is alive.

\*\*\*\*\*

*Alleluia! Lord of life and light and joy, I praise you.*

\*\*\*\*\*

God sometimes speaks to us in strange and surprising ways. Often it seems as though he is not speaking to us at all; he can be silent for a very long time.

When this happens, all we can do is wait patiently and trust, always on the alert for signs of his glory and compassion. Sometimes we are aware of God in the beauty of Nature: a shining river, brilliant stars, Spring flowers, the faces of sleeping children. At other times we may feel his touch in the kindness or understanding of a friend.

It is good to stop sometimes simply to praise God, in prayer, in song or in dance, and to thank him for all that he gives us.

# Born disabled

When Emma was born the doctors expected her to die within hours. She was a very severe case of cerebral palsy and even though she survived the first few days of life nobody thought she would live for as much as a month.

When she was eleven, Emma was sent to a boarding school for disabled children. She could not control her limbs except for her left foot. She could not dress, wash or feed herself and had to spend all her days strapped into a specially made wheelchair. Although she could not exactly speak, she was able to articulate certain sounds in such a way that those closest to her understood her. Sadly many visitors to the school, seeing Emma's limbs thrashing against her chair or hearing the unusual sounds coming from her mouth, looked at her with undisguised pity or furtively moved away. Very few spoke to her directly; most simply assumed that she was also mentally defective.

But through patient, skilful teaching Emma learnt to read, and then there was another breakthrough. She was provided with a high-tech machine, tailored to her needs. By using her controllable left foot she was able to press a switch which activated a typewriter. Almost overnight the school became aware of Emma's vivid, imaginative, and at times wicked sense of humour. She took to writing stories and making jokes and became a "character", much loved and appreciated by her carers and teachers.

One day a number of the school staff fell into a serious discussion. Lessons were over and they were sitting together at one end of a big, and as they thought, an empty classroom. They were talking about the question of allowing severely handicapped newborn babies to survive. Some of them, considering the quality of life of such children and the heavy burden on their parents and siblings, were in favour of letting these infants die naturally.

But suddenly there was a loud shout, and with some dismay the staff realised that Emma had been there all the time, in a far corner of the room hidden behind a cluster of wheelchairs. One of the teachers quickly fetched her to join the group and everyone listened intently as Emma struggled with obvious passion to articulate the words:

"Let them live!"

*****

*Dear Lord, let us beware of any kind of presumption. Help us to give deep and sincere respect to those who are disadvantaged, and to listen to them with open and receptive minds.*

*****

Disability, whether mental or physical, is a huge problem: for those who are disabled, for their families and for society as a whole.

Sometimes disabled children grow up to be a blessing, generating powerful love. Sometimes the parents' marriage breaks up as a result of the strain of caring for such a child, or the other children in the family feel neglected because their handicapped brother or sister needs so much attention. Sometimes the disability is so severe that the sufferer's quality of life seems questionable and sometimes such children, virtually "written off" as babies, turn out to have lively intelligence or a delightful disposition.

In the past, when women gave birth to a handicapped child, they had no option but to try and cope. But nowadays if pregnant women are given a test which shows that their child will be born disabled or deformed, the parents are faced with the terrible choice: whether or not to have an abortion.

It is very important that disabled people are given equivalent rights to the rest of us, the same chance to work, the same opportunities for travel and leisure. It is even more important that as individuals, those of us who are able-bodied treat them as equals, with love and respect.

# Will

Will is a devout Roman Catholic who has lived all his life in the same village where everyone knows him and no news or gossip fails to reach him.

One day he heard that the Anglicans were planning a Rogation Day procession and needed a cross. Without a word to anyone, Will collected his tools, looked out some pieces of wood and in his slow careful way fashioned a large cross. When he had finished he looked at it with a craftsman's pleasure, noting the beauty of the grain and the soft sheen of the wood.

But the cross was plain: there was no figure of Christ nailed to it like the one that hung over Will's mantelpiece. He had decided to go and buy a figure of Jesus, when something made him hesitate.

He remembered that Anglicans generally use plain crosses and thought his gift might be more generous if it did not jar on their sensibilities, or conflict with their ways of worshipping. And as he held his cross in his hands and looked down on it, he thought about Christ crucified, and realised that because his imagination had free rein, the impact the cross made on him was far more effective than that of his crucifix at home. The suffering of Jesus became more real to him as he gazed at the plain cross, the work of his hands.

Will did not take his cross round to the Anglicans

himself. He asked someone to give it to them, and thought that was the end of the matter. But a week or two later, the vicar came round to his cottage and gave him a cheque for fifty pounds.

"We are delighted and grateful for the cross" he said, "and we collected this money for your brother. I believe he is a missionary priest in the Philippines?"

*****

*Lord Jesus, you prayed that we all may be one. Help us to work, in whatever way we can, for the unity of Christians.*

*****

I think there are a lot of people, like Will in the story, quietly beavering away at the cause of Christian Unity. Often, indeed, the actual issue of Unity will be far from their minds; they will simply be working in friendship with other Christians who happen to come from different traditions.

Scholars and theologians are painfully engaged in the long, laborious struggle towards Unity on an academic level, but meanwhile people at the grass roots of society are unobtrusively getting on with living it.

We are no longer so ignorant about one another's denominations, no longer suspicious and fearful about other ways of worshipping God. And what is more, these differences no longer seem to matter very much. What does matter is the peace and goodwill among Christians of all varieties which gives witness to non-believers of the validity and potential of Christ's message.

# Christmas story – 1

Father Joe, a missionary, was home on leave in England. A priest friend, whose mother had been taken seriously ill, had asked him to take over his parish in a pleasant area of the Cotswolds for the Christmas services.

Father Joe arrived in the village on Christmas Eve. As soon as he had put his luggage in the presbytery and made himself a cup of tea, he went to look at the church. It was already dark and there was no-one about. He unlocked the door and went inside, without switching on the lights. There was a soft glow from the sanctuary lamp, but in a side chapel the light was radiant.

Joe moved towards it and discovered a Nativity scene the like of which he had never seen before. A spotlight shone on the life-like doll representing Jesus. He was not lying in a manger, but cradled on his mother's lap, not wrapped in swaddling clothes, but dressed in white satin and lace. The figure of the Virgin was a very beautiful statue, robed in blue and white with a necklace of what looked like pearls and diamonds and a gold ring on her finger. There was a life-size ox and a life-size donkey, both with velvety coats and soulful eyes, and the frame of the crib was decorated with tiny flowers and stars.

For several minutes Joe stood there, gazing down at the crib. He wondered who had made it, who had gone to so much trouble and spent so much money. He thought of the devotion that had gone into making such a splendid crib, in which every detail was beautiful.

He was still contemplating the crib when a memory flashed into his mind, a memory of Manila, exactly two years before. He had gone to the Philippines to seek out and train men to become missionary priests for Africa. One day, just before Christmas, a young man, Thomas, had asked him to accompany him on a walk.

Thomas led him to the place known as Smoky Mountain, an enormous rubbish tip, where many of the poorest lived in terrible poverty. Father Joe followed Thomas across the piles of rubbish and waste, among the makeshift huts, until he stopped outside a shack. Then to the priest's surprise, the young man took off his shoes and motioned him to do the same. It was a sign of reverence; it was what you did before entering a holy place.

The two men went inside and there found a young girl of about thirteen or fourteen, cradling a newborn child in her arms. It was an illumination in all the darkness of poverty and disease around them.

*****

*Lord, I thank you for all the experiences and insights that make us grow in understanding.*

*I thank you for those who willingly give time and energy and money to create something beautiful, in craft or words or music or liturgy, to draw others to you in worship.*

*I thank you also for those whose poverty and simplicity draw us to you as workers in the struggle for justice.*

*****

The crib that Father Joe found in the church may not have been totally "authentic". It seems that whoever made it was carried away by enthusiasm and devotion and lost sight of the bones of the story, forgot that Mary was poor, that the birth of Jesus was messy and hardly respectable. The fantasy of the jewels, flowers and stars was not an accurate representation of what we read in the gospels. But the person who made it may well have been motivated by love, love of God and of all those, especially children, who would come to see the crib.

The child-mother on Smoky Mountain was poor, probably dirty, probably beautiful, as young Filipinos almost invariably are. To the priest and the young man she was a vivid representation of the gospel story, revealing the humanity, vulnerability and poverty of Mary, and reminding them of their call to justice.

# Nameless Hutu

I picked up this story watching television. It was told in seconds, and I could not even catch the man's name. But it is a true story, worth the telling.

The programme, put out on a Saturday night on BBC2, was called "Correspondent". This particular evening, Lindsey Hilsum was reporting on the aftermath of the genocide in Rwanda. It was a story of unredeemed horror and brutality, of man's inhumanity to man. We were told of the Hutus who mercilessly butchered the Tutsis, men, women and children, largely with machetes. Hutus in authority had given orders to ordinary Hutus to kill all the Tutsis they could find.

Then the camera showed us someone standing outside a group of huts. He was a big man, bald, with a moustache. There was nothing remarkable about him. He was a Hutu.

When the order to kill came, this man, whose name I do not know, had refused to obey. Instead, he had hidden seventeen Tutsis and saved their lives.

*****

*Dear Lord, I thank you for the brave-hearted, whose courage and selflessness witness to the glory of the human spirit. May their example inspire us and fill us with hope.*

*****

It is always difficult, even in small things, to stand up and be counted, to speak out against the majority, to act differently from our peers. To do this in life-and-death situations requires someone very special.

I remember thinking, when I saw the Hutu on the television film, that he looked in no way "special". His face, as he spoke simply, was quite undistinguished, and there were no signs of passionate anger or defiance, or indeed pride. Perhaps because he seemed so ordinary, it is appropriate not even to know his name.

And yet this was a man of the stuff of which martyrs are made, though happily he did not die. It was extremely brave to defy the manic authorities who had ordered the butchery of all Tutsis, but what made his courage so exceptional and amazing was the fact that he acted quite alone. Every other Hutu around him was obeying the leaders and hacking their Tutsi neighbours to death; he chose instead to protect them, saving the lives of seventeen Tutsis at obvious risk to his own.

# Zaire

Clare, a mission partner in Zaire, writes as the New Year begins:

"What of those unable to provide for themselves – the children who come to our churches and chapels every morning to get a bowl of soya/maize porridge from our feeding programme? Many are the children of the first wife, abandoned when the husband takes a second or third. When the programme funding runs out later this year, what will happen to them? Are we actually helping them by providing what is only a temporary means of survival, or should we be taking a more long-term view in which they learn to provide for themselves?

"Pray that we may be able to help people recognise their own spiritual needs and find ways to meet them. People are used to crying out to God for material help – there is no-one else! But does God become just another 'aid agency', simply there to provide handouts when the going gets tough? Often material needs are so overwhelming that spiritual life gets buried or for-gotten, even amongst Christians."

*****

*All-loving Father, give us real compassion and care for our brothers and sisters in developing countries. Keep us aware of what is happening in their lives. Enlighten and encourage all those who work to help the underprivileged so that they may feed the hungry, teach the uneducated and bring your goodness, justice, peace and love to all those they meet.*

*****

"I am the bread of life" says Jesus.
"He who comes to me will never be hungry!"
(Jn 6:35)

Jesus is talking here of spiritual hunger, for the longing we all have for fulfilment in peace and love. But we are made up of body, mind, emotions and spirit, all of which are interdependent. When we are deeply unhappy, for example, our physical well-being is affected. And when our bodies cannot function properly, neither can our souls.

For this reason it is not only cruel but quite fruitless to preach the gospel to people who are starving. They must be given bread before they can receive the Bread of Life.

It is for us to feed the hungry and help them to feed themselves. Then they will be ready to hear the Word of God.

# Rita

At the Mass specially arranged for the local Catholic Women's League, the epistle reading happened to be taken from Peter's First Letter, where he says, "Wrap yourselves in humility to be servants of each other" (1 Pet 5:5).

The priest, beginning his homily, said, with feeling, that he had no intention of exhorting the women present to be humble, because for centuries women have been treated as servants and indeed sometimes as slaves.

I thought of Rita, my servant in India. We lived there some years after India had gained her independence from the British, and in our remote part of South India, the old imperial system still prevailed. My husband and I, young, strong and healthy and in my case not working, had eight servants to look after us.

This is not quite as absurd as it sounds. If we had not given them employment they would have had no work, and under the caste system there is a strict code governing what sort of work a particular person may do. So we had a head boy, a cook, a driver, a night-watchman, two gardeners, a sweeper and a dhobi who did the laundry.

When our first son was born we added a ninth, Rita, the ayah, or children's nurse.

It was a happy household and everyone seemed to get along well. I led an idyllic life, playing with my babies but never washing their nappies.

Then one day Rita fainted. When she came to she admitted that she had not eaten anything for days. She began to cry and told us that her own five children were desperately hungry because her husband had taken all the money and spent it on drink. Of course we were appalled. Deeply ashamed that I had failed to realise what was going on, I took out my purse, gave Rita a handful of rupee notes, and packed her off home to feed herself and her children and rest for a few days.

Rita always wore a plain white cotton sari which looked fresh and clean, so you can imagine my surprise when she came back to work in a gold-bordered rose pink sari made from some flimsy material. Her face was alight with pleasure and pride but I responded coldly. I had given her money for her starving children. What right had she to spend any of it on this gaudy garment for herself?

When Rita washed the new sari the pink and gold disappeared. Sadly she hung the faded cloth out to dry and the cheap fabric simply disintegrated.

Did I think "Serve her right!"? Or was I sorry for her? After all these years I cannot remember. But I hope I was sorry, and showed it. After all, I had a wardrobe full of dresses. How could I have begrudged Rita her one act of self-indulgence?

*****

*Lord Jesus, you gave us an example of service when you washed the feet of your disciples. Help us to be ready to reverence and to serve all those who cross our path.*

*****

I failed completely to stand in Rita's shoes. Instead I was quick to judge her, without knowing all the circumstances, without knowing how she felt.

Probably it was particularly difficult for me because of the difference in our cultures, but I am afraid I continue to make the same mistakes, to criticise what other people do or say without even trying to get under their skin, to understand what it is like to be them in their situation.

Jesus urged us to love our enemies, for most of us a very tall order indeed. But if we can make a real effort to understand the motives and compulsions of those who irritate or annoy us, if we sincerely pray for them, we will surely find the number of our "enemies" decreasing fast.

# Megan's story

At the moment Tony is the biggest thorn in my flesh. He's nearly fifteen now, and we adopted him when he was four. He's a big lad (he towers over me and I'm no midget) and his face would be handsome if it didn't perpetually wear an expression of sullen animosity.

I couldn't honestly say that Tony has an attractive personality – he is surly, vindictive, glum and aggressive. I know about adolescents, having endured four before him, but compared to Tony they were sweetness and light.

Most of his present hate and anger is directed towards me. The psychiatrist who keeps our heads above water tells me this is because I'm the most important person in his life – small comfort when he has deliberately tipped out the entire contents of my one-and-only bottle of expensive scent, or showered a carton of cornflakes over our living-room carpet. He accompanies these actions with a stream of obscene, blasphemous and meaningless abuse, together with threats of what he would like to do to me – none of them very nice. I've heard people speak of a hot-tempered person having a short fuse – well poor old Tony doesn't seem to have any fuse at all.

And the positive side? Well, there just isn't one, at least I didn't think there was. He never does anything to help, never shows any consideration or appreciation, and sadly, never smiles.

In recent months he's developed a new line of attack. "Why do you have to be so religious?" he asked. "Why do I have to have a nutter for a mother when other people have normal ones?" He hid my prayer book and bible, took down a lovely print of the Nativity from my bedroom wall, and threw my wooden cross into the bin.

At first I thought he was just sticking the knife in where he knew it would hurt. But when one day he said, literally pleading with me for once, "If you give up religion I would do without a birthday present", I knew there was more to it than that. I think Tony sees himself as belonging to despised minorities – he's adopted and he goes to a special school. And so he wants to be as normal and conforming as possible in every way he can, even down to the way his parents spend their leisure time. But I told him firmly that I couldn't give up on God, not even for him, and he went away sadly.

Then I was taken ill, so ill that my husband called the doctor, an unheard-of thing in our house. One afternoon as I lay in bed, half-conscious, the bedroom door was opened more noisily than usual. I kept quite still with my eyes shut. Tony approached the bed and then nothing happened for a long time until I felt his hand on my head, gently stroking me in something between a benediction and a caress. He lifted up the sheet and thrust something under it.

Hours later I felt something pricking uncomfortably at my side. I felt for it and drew it up to the light. It was made of cheap metal and imitation mother-of-pearl. It was a crucifix – a gift of love if ever I received one.

*****

*Lord Jesus, help us to see you in one another. Let us never give up on people, however difficult and destructive they seem.*

*****

Sometimes people surprise us. The ones we have written off as hopeless, useless or worse, suddenly reveal some hidden quality that redeems them in our eyes. Tony was not so bad after all – indeed he showed both thoughtfulness and compassion.

We need to be wary of expecting the worst of people. We will be far happier if we look for the best in them.

# Verity's story

My eyes were opened last weekend when we went to visit our son in London.

Tom and I are not particularly successful and we're certainly not rich, but now in middle age we're reasonably comfortable and we live where we choose to live, in a small village called Edenfield in the middle of the country. We like all that goes with this: wild flowers, birdsong, trees and hills and quiet, but what means far more to us is our good fortune in living in a real community. We all know one another. Depending on your temperament you are either irritated or amused to discover that everybody else seems to know what you're doing before you know it yourself. But even the easily irritated are grateful when they're ill, stuck in the snow, stranded with a car that won't budge, or in need of a shoulder to cry on, to find that there's always someone ready to help.

Last weekend we went to visit our son Matt who lives in a less-than-salubrious part of London, south of the river. He is young and hard-up; his bed-sit is cheerful but looks out onto a grim street where the gutters are full of litter and the people look weary and dejected. There's the non-stop roar of traffic and not a tree in sight. I felt sorry for Matt, surrounded by poverty and grime, and most of all for what I guessed to be a rootless, impersonal, cheerless existence. But I was wrong.

In the evening he invited us to come with him to his local. I didn't really want to go – (in my mind's eye I saw our village pub, its beautiful stonework and leafy courtyard) – but I entered the mock-Tudor monstrosity with teeth gritted and a determined smile. It was all predictable: noisy, crowded, with a deafening jukebox, lots of imitation brasses, and an artificial log fire. I felt sorry not just for my son but for all the others who sought entertainment and consolation there.

Matt introduced us to the landlord, Bill, but after a few minutes he apologised and said he had to leave for an hour. When he'd gone, Matt explained that he went every evening to visit a customer, an old man who lived by himself and who had had a severe stroke. When Bill came back from the hospital, a little round Cockney woman came up and began to consult him earnestly about a family down the road who were having a difficult time. I listened and said nothing.

On the way home Matt said, "Bill's a good guy. He drove me to work when I overslept last week. And May his wife insists on doing my ironing. They're all good around here: old Charlie fixed my electric fire when it bust…"

I was delighted. "Why, Matt", I said, "it sounds like home!" Matt looked blank for a moment. "Home?" he said. Then he looked embarrassed. "Sorry Mum, but this is home to me now. I know it's not Edenfield, but well…" he faltered. I knew he was afraid we'd be hurt.

Tom smiled. "Don't worry Matt", he said. "You've got a great home here. You don't have to live in a cosy little place like Edenfield to feel you belong."

We were glad to come home to the peace and beauty of our village, but glad too that Matt has found his own community in the back streets of south London.

*****

*Lord Jesus, I ask for myself and for all your chil-
dren, that each of us may have a sense of belonging
to a community, of being a part of something greater
than ourselves, of drawing support from and giving
support to those among whom we live.*

*****

We all need to be part of a community. It may be our family, the regulars at our pub, the people in our street, the people we work with, our parish. In community we give and take, support and are supported, learn and teach.

Some people, aware that the old patterns of society are breaking up and families are scattered, choose to join an official, structured community where they live together with a group of others, usually united by a common purpose.

Such communities often thrive, because of the good-will of the members and their determination to suc-ceed in their life together. But it is not easy to live in this way because communities are not natural in the way that a family is. People come together as strangers, committed it is true to an ideal: of Christianity, per-haps, or simple living, but challenged also to weather all the tensions between personalities that will inevita-bly arise.

# Bad name

When two Little Sisters of Jesus came to live in the town the Council offered them a house in the notorious housing estate called Larkfields. It was the place where most of the local problem families lived. Drug and alcohol abuse and every sort of crime were said to be rife there.

Sister Agnes and Sister Rose were happy to make this their home and soon settled in. Agnes worked in the local factory and Rose got a job cleaning in the hospital. Gradually they began to befriend their neighbours and they soon learnt that Nancy who lived in the house opposite had a bad name in the estate where she was universally despised and distrusted. Nancy was an alcoholic given to swearing and physical violence. Her daughter had committed suicide, her son was in prison.

The two Sisters often prayed for Nancy and talked about her, wondering how they could befriend and help her, but the task seemed daunting. Then one winter Saturday, when they had been in the town about six months, they came home exhausted after a day giving a party for disabled people in the Day Centre. When they stepped off the bus, it was raining heavily.

"Have you eaten anything all day?" asked Rose.

"There wasn't time" said Agnes.

"I know. But I'm ravenous now – and I'm sorry, Agnes, but I forgot to stock up – "

Inside their kitchen they found the larder empty except for a small can of baked beans. Rose was just about to open it when there was a knock at the door.

There stood Nancy, fat, unkempt but smiling.

"How would you like to come over to my house?" she said, "I've made a hotpot and an apple pie. I know you've been at the Day Centre all day and you must be exhausted – "

*****

*Lord, save us from judging. Save us from thinking of ourselves as the ones who must always give. Teach us to receive with humility and joy.*

*****

It is not very clear from this story why Nancy had such a bad reputation, just as it is not clear in the gospels why Mary Magdalene had a bad name.

Both these women acted in ways that were completely unexpected. Mary Magdalene's penitence was all the more moving because it came as a surprise if not a shock to the people who were present. Nancy's warming hospitality was all the more appreciated because it was seemingly out of character.

No-one deserves to be given a "bad name", because none of us is in a position to know what another person is really like. All of us have hidden qualities, good and bad, and perhaps sometimes those whose failings are very obvious are also the ones who are capable of great generosity and compassion.

# Ex-prisoner of war

Early in 1995 the government was making plans for the fiftieth anniversary, on May 8th, of the end of the Second World War in Europe. The Germans had been officially invited and this has brought into discussion the question of VJ Day, which marked the end of hostilities against Japan. That fiftieth anniversary was to be marked in August 1995 and it had already been decided that the Japanese would not be invited to take part in the official ceremonies. There was still so much bitter anger against the Japanese for their brutal treatment of prisoners-of-war. Survivors and families of survivors found it impossible to forgive.

But not all of them. I was talking with a friend whose father, Mark John Kennaway, was in the notorious Changi prison camp for three and a half years. She told me that he came home to his family on a stretcher weighing just five stone.

My friend said, "We never really found out very much about the worst things that went on in Changi, because he always used to laugh and say he'd had a very nice peaceful time and no school fees to pay for his children."

From what we know of Changi, it seems clear that this man was putting on a brave face in order to protect his wife and daughters from realising the full horrors of his life in the camp.

But his daughter also told me that he was able completely to forgive the Japanese for everything they had done to him.

I thought of Mark Kennaway when, at the end of the VJ celebrations, a survivor of the atrocities in Burma was asked for his most vivid memory of that time. The man thought for a moment and then he said, "The butterflies".

\*\*\*\*\*

*Lord, sometimes it is very hard to forgive, impossible even. Help us not to judge people who find they cannot bring themselves to show mercy to those who have inflicted great suffering on them or on those they love. But help us also to be inspired by the merciful.*

\*\*\*\*\*

For most of us, forgiveness does not come easy. There are outstanding examples of forgiveness.

Jesus dying on the cross, said, "Father, forgive them; they do not know what they are doing" (Lk 23:34).

The last words of Stephen, who was stoned to death because he was a follower of Jesus, were "Lord, do not hold this sin against them" (Acts 7:60).

And this prayer was found in a concentration camp where thousands of women and children had been killed:

Remember, Lord,
not just the men and women of goodwill
but also those of ill will,

not just our suffering –
but also the fruits of this suffering –
our comradeship, loyalty, humility,
courage, generosity and greatness of heart,
which has grown out of all this.
And when they come to judgement,
let all the fruits that we have borne,
be their forgiveness.   (Anon.)

But most of us cannot aspire to such greatness of heart, and it is not for us, who have only had to forgive small hurts, to condemn others whose experience is different from ours. The mother of the little girl murdered long ago cannot bring herself to forgive. Many war veterans cannot bring themselves to forgive the Japanese. And since we cannot understand what it was like for them, we have no right to judge their unforgivingness.

Yet even so we can wonder at the generosity of spirit of those rare beings like Mark John Kennaway, who, when he was asked about the torture, starvation, disease and death in the camp at Changi, was able to smile.

# Judy

Judy suffered an appalling childhood. Her parents, of mixed race, were incapable of looking after her so the authorities took her into Care. After a few years a couple were allowed to adopt her and this seemed like a happy ending. But by the time Judy was eleven, the adoptive couple were both abusing her and her "father" began to rape her on an almost daily basis.

Judy escaped from this family and began living on the streets. Quickly she drifted into prostitution but at the age of seventeen sought help. She went to a hostel for street people run by Christians and there she met Kath who was possibly the first truly loving person Judy had ever known.

Under Kath's influence Judy began to change. She started to feel positive about life and decided to pull herself out of the miserable, degrading, violent situation in which she had lived for so long. She began to study and with Kath's help and a lot of determination eventually succeeded in finding a job and an apartment of her own.

Now Judy is in her mid-twenties. What kind of person has emerged from the trauma of such a childhood and adolescence? We might expect her to be immoral, or amoral, concerned for no-one but herself. We might expect her to be bitter.

But Judy is none of these things. After a long struggle with the authorities she has been given permission to foster three young children, an eleven-year-old girl and a younger girl and boy. All are of mixed race as Judy is, all have been deprived of love as she was.

*****

*Lord, when I hear of people like Judy I understand that there is hope in our world. Help me to keep on believing in this, and in the power of love such as Kath's.*

*****

When I first heard about Judy's childhood I was shocked and horrified. Like everyone else, I have been through "bad times and good times", but Judy's experience is so far removed from my own that I cannot even imagine what it was like for her.

And then, when I heard what sort of adult she had become: warm, compassionate, affectionate, I was amazed and full of admiration.

That is how I felt, and still do. But when I spent some time thinking about Judy, I realised that some of my own theories had received a jolting. So often I have tried to persuade people to take a more lenient attitude towards offenders of various kinds, asking how can we expect people who have suffered traumatic childhoods to behave as exemplary citizens. But the story of Judy seems to give the lie to this. She endured prolonged neglect, cruelty and abuse as a child; now she is herself giving love and hope and a future to three deprived children.

If we look more closely at Judy's story we can find a

clue which probably explains why she has become the generous, stable woman she is. At the age of seventeen she looked for help and found it. Since then she has received the constant, faithful love and support of Kath and another friend. They believe in Judy, and she has not let them down.

Before I knew this story, I would have doubted that it could happen. I think I might have said, "Seventeen is much too old for any hope of transformation." But I have met Judy, and I know it can be done.

# Christmas story – 2

I was very surprised, at first, when Peg told me she hated Christmas, because she is as good a Christian as I know. Every Christmas Day she goes to church and celebrates the great feast with the people in her parish, rejoicing in the birth of God's Son into our world.

It is the time afterwards that Peg hates, or used to hate, the time for the family, for presents round the tree, turkey and all the trimmings. The reason for this is simple: Peg has no family now and deeply unhappy memories of the family she once had.

When I realised that she was lonely and unhappy at this time, I made up my mind to telephone her each year on Christmas Day. And last year, everything was different. Peg was not alone; there was a tree in her house with presents under it, and there had been a big meal with turkey and all the trimmings.

Peg explained. She is a regular visitor at the local prison. For financial reasons, the whole prison closed down last year for a whole week over Christmas and all the prisoners were sent home. All, that is, except two, who had no home to go to. There are no prizes for guessing who invited them to spend Christmas with her.

George and Bernard could scarcely believe their luck. They had a wonderful time. When they were relaxing after the meal, Bernard told Peg he was thirty-five years old, "And this is the first real Christmas I ever had" he added.

Peg told me all this on the telephone, and then she added, "I don't hate Christmas any more."

*****

*Lord, empower us with courage and generosity. Let us be welcoming to all who need our hospitality, and open our eyes to see that goodness and joy can come from unexpected sources.*

*****

It happens quite often that joy comes when we are trying to give joy to others. Peg set out to give the two prisoners a happy Christmas and was surprised to find herself enjoying the day too.

Peg is a prison visitor because she wants to bring comfort and cheer to prisoners. She feels sorry for most of those who are condemned to life in jail, separated as they are from those they love and in some cases victims of bullying in prison.

Many other people have a very different attitude. They are angry because prisons are becoming more comfortable. Some exaggerate bitterly, saying "They are like 5-star hotels, a television in every cell." It is not difficult to understand the anger of someone whose old mother has been battered to death or whose daughter has been raped. They cry out for vengeance: prison is the punishment and must be a punishment.

But the majority of prisoners are not murderers or rapists. They may deserve punishment for the crimes they have committed; they also need rehabilitation.

Very often prisoners are themselves victims of the society they have grown up in. They may be the sons and grandsons or sisters and daughters of criminals. A considerable proportion of prisoners are alcoholics, driven to stealing by their addiction, or mentally unstable people hardly responsible for their actions.

Perhaps we should ask: do we want people to emerge from our prisons bitter, brutalised, more skilled in crime, or better educated, determined to "go straight", with confidence in their future?

In Matthew's gospel, Jesus paints a picture of the Last Judgement. He says, "Come, you whom my Father has blessed, take for your heritage the Kingdom prepared for you... For I was hungry and you gave me food ... sick and you visited me, in prison and you came to see me" (Mt 25:34-36).

I think Peg is one of those whom the Father has blessed.

# Lady in Liberia

A missionary priest, Father Pat Kelly, was at one time parish priest in a wealthy city in Liberia, where a large proportion of his parishioners were white diplomats and professional people.

One Sunday as he was about to begin his sermon, a black woman wearing trousers (a thing not approved of in that society) stood up and walked to the front of the church. She said "I want to talk."

Father Pat said, gently, "Yes, yes, afterwards."

"No," said the woman, "I want to speak now."

Father Pat was embarrassed. He said, "Are there any members of the Parish Council here?" hoping that someone would come forward and pacify her. But of course no-one did. So having no alternative, he indicated to the woman that she could speak.

Facing the congregation, she spoke clearly. "I am a beggar" she said. "I sit every day outside the supermarket. I know a lot of your faces, but you always pass me by, you never give me anything. I am not asking you for anything today, only to answer one question. What I want to know is, 'Why do you come here, to church?'" Then she sat down.

Father Pat said "I am not going to preach today. Our sister has done it for me. Let us spend some time in silence, thinking about what she has said."

\*\*\*\*\*

*Lord, keep us awake and sensitive to the needs and the feelings of others.*

\*\*\*\*\*

I love this story for several reasons. First because the priest who told it to me was there when it happened and was quite shaken by the experience, secondly because I like to imagine the drama of the scene and its effect on the congregation, thirdly because I know I would not in a million years have had the guts of that African woman to stand up and say what she did. Last, and most importantly, I like this story because the woman was so right to question the thinking of people who went to church on Sunday but failed to give to those in need.

# Hero

Sometimes it only needs one man or woman to bring about a major transformation for the good of humanity by a single act of courage.

Such a man is Ray Hamley, a retired schoolteacher. He fought in the Second World War as a navigator/bombardier in the R.A.F. One night in 1944, when he was about twenty years old, Ray's plane scored a direct hit on a church during a raid on the small German town of Kleve. The church was destroyed. There was no-one inside it, but many people living nearby were killed. When Ray looked down on the havoc he had caused he felt a glow of satisfaction; it was a job well done.

But gradually, as the years went by, Ray's attitude changed. Instead of feeling proud of what he had done, he started to feel concerned, worried and then guilty and ashamed. The memory of that particular "successful" raid began to haunt him.

It took a long time and a lot of courage, but at last, when he was sixty years old, Ray sat down and wrote a letter to the Burgermeister of Kleve, explaining who he was and asking for forgiveness for what he had done.

The letter was passed to the priest of the church which had by now been rebuilt. The priest read Ray's letter to all his congregations at the Sunday Masses. He told the people that he had written to Ray, saying that he personally forgave him. His letter was at the back of the church, left open for anyone who wanted to add their signature. By the end of the day several hundred people had signed the letter. It was posted to Ray, and arrived on his birthday.

The story does not end here. Ray accepted an invitation to visit the people of Kleve, and from that small beginning a strong friendship has grown up between the two towns, and the spirit of reconciliation flourishes in the good will of ordinary Germans and ordinary Yorkshire folk towards each other.

*****

*Lord, give us the wisdom to understand ourselves, the determination to seek forgiveness when we need it and the courage to take risks for your sake and for the sake of our fellow men and women.*

*****

Not everyone has the same idea of what a hero is. It seems likely that when the young airman, Ray Hamley, returned home after his successful bombing raids in the Second World War, he was hailed as a hero by his family and friends. Undoubtedly, he was a brave young man.

But in my opinion he was even braver as an old man. It takes a good deal of courage to ask forgiveness of those whose loved ones you were responsible for killing. And it takes extra courage to do this alone, as Ray did.

It was a heroic act, even as the generosity of those who forgave so freely was heroic. And the first fruit of

this heroism is the reconciliation and growing friendship between peoples who once regarded each other
with suspicion and hatred.

For this achievement Ray has won no medal. What
he has won is the love and gratitude of two communities.

# Petra's story

Jack came into my life one late November night, and went out of it two hours later.

I used to do voluntary duty at a shelter for the homeless. We didn't actually provide accommodation; we just welcomed people with a cup of tea and let them talk and get a bit of warmth. There was normally a man on duty at night-time, but this particular night my partner was taken ill at the last moment. I could have phoned for a substitute, but I reckoned I could manage on my own. There didn't seem to be anything happening and I had a good book which I was enjoying. I was due to be relieved at midnight.

Just before ten, I opened the door to Jack. As soon as I saw him I wished I hadn't, I wished I'd remembered to put the chain across. He had a dead-white face with a sort of twisted look about it that looked sinister to me. I know if I had seen Jack coming along the street towards me, even in daylight, my instinct would have been to cross over to the other side.

I led him to the interview room, and got him to sit down. Then I made us a cup of tea and sat opposite him. All the time I was praying feverishly inside – "God, help me to cope with this, please!" and at the same time on the outside I was trying to seem calm and receptive.

After a few sips of hot, sweet tea, Jack began to talk. From time to time he put his hands in the pockets of his filthy overcoat, rummaging for something. I kept expecting him to pull out a knife, but the only thing he eventually drew out was the most revolting handkerchief imaginable.

As Jack talked, we both began to relax. Now I was silently asking something else of God: "Please let your love reach him through me." At first I had been terrified, but my fear changed to dismay and then, pity. Slowly as I listened, I began to feel real concern for him

Jack is a compulsive child-abuser; he has been in prison many times. He's also an alcoholic and a depressive. Perhaps he should be locked away. As it is, he has nowhere to lay his head, or so he feels, because the police, quite understandably, are on the look-out for him in whichever city he tries to hide. He has no family, no friends, anywhere.

In the middle of his story he suddenly said, "I believe in God."

"So do I" I said. It was almost the first time I had spoken, and it was the first, if not the only thing we had in common.

"You may think I'm terrible for this, you may be disgusted with me, but God isn't disgusted. The only place I can find when I really want to pray is the public lavatories. I expect you're shocked. But he isn't. I know he listens to me."

Just before midnight Dave arrived to relieve me. He's kind-hearted and hard-headed, vastly more experienced in the way of dossers than me. He sized up the situation in seconds.

"It's time you were on your way, old man" he said, not unkindly but with the authority that men like Jack are quick to recognise. "Just a minute, please, Dave" I said, resenting this abrupt end to our time together, "could I have a few more words with Jack before he goes?"

Dave left us and Jack stood up. He was a desperately unhappy man, with nothing to live for and no-one to care about him, but he made one of the most courteous speeches I have ever heard, thanking me for listening and trusting him. I went over to shake hands, but at the last minute some impulse made me kiss him gently on the cheek.

Having heard the story of his life, I can't help wondering if it was the first kiss he had ever received, and I'm very much afraid it was the last. He went out into the night and I never saw him again.

*****

*Compassionate Lord, help us to see with your eyes and hear with your ears, never judging our brothers and sisters.*

*****

When child molesters or alleged child molesters are taken to court, crowds gather to hurl abuse at them. Perhaps there is no section of the community which attracts more hatred and anger.

The abuse of young children is a horrific crime and it is hard to find any pity for the perpetrators. Perhaps we can begin to understand, and therefore to judge less harshly, when we realise that such people are usually sick, that their actions spring not so much from wickedness as from a compulsion which they cannot control.

However that may be, Petra in the story was drawn to feel real compassion for Jack.

# Little Sister

On a weekend course I met a friendly nun, a Little Sister of Jesus called Martha.

The convent where the course was held was some distance out of London and far from any railway station or bus route. Realising this, I had arranged for my son John to come and fetch me and drive me to his house in one of London's leafier suburbs.

After lunch on the Sunday, people were busy organizing their departures and I noticed Sister Martha looking pensive rather than purposeful.

"How are you getting home, Sister?" I asked.

She smiled. "Well, I hadn't really thought about that," she said, "I have to get back to London somehow."

John is a kind son, well used to his mother's unpredictable ways, so I knew there would be no problem. By two o'clock Sister Martha and I were comfortably installed in the back of his car.

John is a detective sergeant working with the Metropolitan Police and he was not fazed by Martha's somewhat vague directions. I began to feel rather concerned as we drew nearer to her home. We were in one of those desolate parts of London where there are no trees, but litter in all the gutters and many boarded-up shops. Aggressive-looking youths hung around street corners and a few old people shuffled along the pavements looking apathetic and depressed.

I wondered about Sister Martha. Was it safe for her living here?

"Are you afraid to go out at night on your own?" I asked her.

She looked at me in surprise, as if she was thinking, What a silly question! But she just smiled and said, "No!"

We left her to make her way up to the fourteenth floor of the high-rise building where she lives with two of her Sisters. As we drove away, John, who is six foot four and hefty with it, and has been officially commended for bravery, said to me:

"I wouldn't want to walk on those streets alone, not even in daylight."

*****

*Lord, I thank you for Sister Martha and all those like her who not only side with the poor but identify with them, sharing their lives, eating and drinking and working with them, suffering and rejoicing with them.*

*Keep me from the danger of staying within the confines of my own comfortable community. Let me go out to meet others who come from different backgrounds and live in different circumstances, so that I may give to them and receive from them an exchange of love, in imitation of your Son, our Lord Jesus Christ.*

*****

I have known a lot of good people, Christians among them. I have known contemplative nuns, who have given their lives to prayer, especially intercession for others. I have known missionaries who have left everything familiar to go and preach the good news of Jesus in lands far away. I have been inspired by excellent writers and preachers, and impressed by the devotion to God and to others of various teachers and nurses and social workers and ordinary folk.

And thinking about all of these good men and women, it seems to me that those who live closest to Jesus Christ and are most like him, are the ones who choose to live like he did. He came voluntarily into our messy violent world and lived among us, caring about the poor and the disadvantaged. The Little Sisters and Brothers of Jesus and the Salvation Army, so very different in their traditions, choose to live among the poor, and more importantly, to share their lives.

# Alé:
# bee-keeper and theologian

Alé comes from Lithuania. She grew up in the country, where her father worked as a forester. Under the Communist regime the family continued to worship God and to go to church, a practice frowned upon by the authorities.

Alé and her twin brother were very bright children, but because they were known to be Christians, they were penalized at school. However good their work was, they were given low marks by the teachers. The other children, who were not Christians, saw the unfairness of this and sympathised.

Eventually Alé's brother became so discouraged that he gave up trying. But she persevered, and when she was eighteen she applied to go to university. She was laughed at and told that she had no chance of a university education, so instead she did a two-year training in bee-keeping. She qualified, and worked as a bee-keeper for eighteen months before taking another course in librarianship.

Then independence came to Lithuania, and Alé's life changed dramatically. She was admitted to university to study theology.

Alé has a bright, happy smile. She is twenty-eight

years old, but she looks about twenty. She also looks like a fresh-faced country girl, and seeing her, it's hard to believe that she is a student of theology. It is also hard to believe how much she has suffered and struggled.

*****

*Dear Lord, I thank you for all those who like Alé overcome grave difficulties by their bravery and determination. I pray for all who are persecuted for their beliefs, and I thank you for the freedom I have to worship you without fear.*

*****

When the Soviet Union broke up, small countries like Lithuania rejoiced in their freedom and independence, and we in the West rejoiced with them. In the years since then a number of serious problems have come to light, social, economic and political. Sadly many people in the newly independent countries are attracted to some of the worst aspects of western life, especially materialism. But for Christians in these countries there is new-found liberation and opportunity.

# Bail hostel

Fran often asked herself 'Where did I go wrong?' when she thought, as she did every day, of her son Charlie.

As far as she could tell he had been brought up in exactly the same way as his older brother and sister. Yet John was about to qualify as a doctor, and Anna was happily married, expecting her first baby, whereas Charlie had left home at sixteen. Homeless and jobless, he had drifted into drugs and then crime.

Two weeks ago he had been caught breaking into a warehouse – by no means his first offence, and now he was in a bail hostel somewhere in London waiting for his case to be brought to court. He had phoned Fran to tell her this, but refused to give her his address.

She longed to see Charlie again, to give him a hug, to take him some money. But it was no use; for some reason he didn't want to see her. Fran loved Charlie, she prayed for him every morning and every night, and before she went to sleep she often wept, wondering where he was, if he was all right, wishing she could hold him as she had held him when he was a little boy. She was crying herself to sleep one night when the telephone rang. It was Charlie, and he sounded frightened.

"Mum," he said, "Mum, listen. You've got to get me out of here."

"Oh Charlie," Fran said, "you know I can't do that, love. If you run away from the bail hostel you'll end up in prison, and that would be worse."

"No, it wouldn't, Mum." Charlie sounded desperate. "You don't know what it's like in here. There's this big guy. He's got a gang and he keeps threatening me with his knife. He's already slashed me once and he says he'll carve my face up if I don't give him my watch – you know, the one you gave me. Mum, please!"

"Oh Charlie" Fran felt desperate herself, "can't you tell the staff, the people in charge? Would you like me to tell them?"

"NO!" Charlie shouted, panic in his voice now. "You don't understand. They'd kill me if I grassed on them. No, just get me out of here, please I beg you, Mum!"

"But Charlie," Fran began, "I can't – "

Charlie swore and put the phone down.

\*\*\*\*\*

*Lord Jesus, I pray for all those who grieve over their children, and all those who suffer from needless guilt.*

*Increase our awareness of what is happening in our society, and give us the courage to take action wherever we find injustice.*

\*\*\*\*\*

A young friend of mine who had been in trouble with the law once or twice told me that he would far rather be in prison than in a bail hostel.

"I was on remand for nearly a year" he said, "for something I hadn't done, and the four months I spent in prison were paradise compared with that hostel. People could get away with murder, and I dare say some did. If you were there with one of those really tough men you were at their mercy. The staff could do nothing. It's not something a lot of people know about."

I for one hadn't known anything about bail hostels, but I certainly understood the grief and frustration of Charlie's mother.

# The dregs

When Heather was offered a supply teaching job at the primary school in her own neighbourhood, she hesitated. She was reluctant to find herself teaching her own son, Bobby.

Bobby was eight and a half and still unable to read. He had a sunny disposition and loved animals and music and every sort of physical activity, but there was no doubt he was slow at all his lessons. Heather knew from parent evenings that his class teacher Mrs Norton could be pretty scathing about poor achievers, and she was afraid that her protective feelings towards Bobby might get out of hand if she was working in the same school.

But with her husband out of work, and three other children to support, Heather needed the money badly and so she decided to take the job.

At first all went well. She hardly saw Bobby, except when he was out in the playground, and it was easy to see he was popular there.

Then one afternoon at breaktime Jennifer Norton, Bobby's class teacher, began talking enthusiastically about the play she was putting on at the end of the term.

"It's called 'Over the Rainbow'" she said "and there are four wonderful parts in it for the bright kids. I've got little Tommy Clough for the West Wind – that's a funny part – and Susie Jessop will be Sunshine. Can't you just see her? She'll look lovely – "

"I know that play" said Helen Brown, the deputy head. "You're right, Jennifer, its very colourful and there are a lot of really good parts. The only thing is, who can you get to be the Rain? That's a really deary part for three poor youngsters!"

Mrs Norton laughed.

"Yes, I know. I've already cast the Rain. I'm giving it to the Macdonald twins and Bobby Linaker – you know, the dregs."

\*\*\*\*\*

*Lord, save us from putting labels on people,*
*from putting them into neat categories,*
*and from putting them down.*

\*\*\*\*\*

To stick labels on people, to categorize them as "Dregs", "Sloanes", "Lefties" or "Yobs" is to deny their uniqueness. It is tantamount to saying they are not persons in their own right but just part of a "job lot".

Usually, too, such labels are both derogatory and judgemental. It must be hurtful and embarrassing for someone to be labelled "Essex man", with its implications of mediocrity, simply because he happened to be born in that county.

But what happened at the school in Heather's story is worse than this. To categorize children as dregs is to suggest that they are worthless, without attractiveness or potential of any kind, and it is sad that a teacher showed such insensitivity.

Nowadays in our education system there is often a dangerous overemphasis on academic attainment, dangerous because it means that children's other gifts, such as creativity, physical skills, spontaneity or thoughtfulness receive little recognition or are positively discouraged. Yet a child who has difficulty in reading, writing and arithmetic may well be a delightful person, full of promise.

# Learning from Paddy

When Dorothy Glyn retired, after forty years of teaching, her life was blessedly peaceful. Now she had much more time to do the things she enjoyed doing: reading, listening to music, walking in the countryside. She became an active member of a Peace Group, and best of all she had time to think.

In these later years of her life Dorothy became a pacifist. She was strongly opposed to violence in every form. And when she looked back over her long years in schools, she thought with horror of the times she had seen children caned, often for such small misdemeanours as being late or forgetting their spellings. And then she remembered with shame that she herself had not always refrained from physical punishment.

A picture flashed into her mind: the face of Paddy Blake. It was a round, freckled face with a cheeky expression. Paddy had been a difficult child, disruptive in every lesson, defiant and disobedient. More than once Dorothy had hit him across the knuckles with a ruler, and although she still could not think of any other way she could have controlled the little boy, her face burned at the memory.

Paddy had lived in a Home because he had been abandoned by his parents. He had grown more difficult as he grew older and when he was ten those in charge of him felt no longer able to cope and he was sent away to another establishment. Dorothy had not thought of him for a very long time, and it was at least twenty years since she had seen him.

Not long after this disturbing memory, she answered a knock on her door and found a tall, strong-looking fellow beaming down at her. She had no idea who it could be, but the young man seemed very pleased to see her.

"You don't remember me, do you, Miss Glyn?" he said, "Paddy Blake!"

Dorothy did not have to pretend to be delighted to see him. He came in and stayed for about an hour, chatting easily about the old days and then talking about his present life. Dorothy warmed to him. He looked slightly scruffy but not dirty; he had got a job that sounded more or less permanent as a hotel porter. He was relaxed and confident: there were no signs of nervousness.

Dorothy was glad that he had come to see her, and told him so as he got up to leave. Then he did a most surprising thing. He bent down and kissed her.

She felt humble and grateful. She thought: many years ago I hurt a child, and now he has come back as a man, a man whom not many people think of as a good person, and given me a sign of love.

*****

*Lord, God of surprises, keep us ever ready to learn from one another.*

*****

We can all learn from all sorts of unexpected people, as the teacher in the story learnt from her pupil. Many who go out to developing countries to help the poor find their lives enormously enriched by the disadvantaged underprivileged people among whom they are working. If we keep our eyes and ears and especially our minds, alert and open, there are opportunities all around us for learning, for increasing our knowledge, experience and awareness.

# Crowds

Jess invited her friend Kathleen to come to stay with her for a few days. Kathleen had recently been divorced and Jess hoped that the visit would be refreshing and enjoyable.

Kathleen arrived late one evening, and after a couple of hours' conversation asked to be excused because she was tired after the journey and went to bed.

Next morning Jess was elated to find that it was warm and sunny. It was early April and she had planned to take Kathleen to a narrow valley some twenty miles away where at this time of year many thousands of wild daffodils were to be seen in bloom. Kathleen was delighted at this suggestion.

"What a lovely idea!" she said, "You've remembered how much I love the countryside, and especially wild flowers."

But when they arrived at the valley, Kathleen's face fell. There were thousands of daffodils, yes, but there were also hundreds of people.

"I hate crowds!" she said.

Jess had difficulty persuading Kathleen to take the walk along the bank of the little stream where the daffodils grew. Eventually she agreed, but instead of gazing at the beauty of the flowers and the stream and the still-bare trees, she seemed intent on criticising everything and everyone.

"Did you see that child?" she asked angrily. "He just threw his coca-cola tin among the flowers! And look at those ridiculous women, so unsuitably dressed. Their high heels are already covered in mud – serve them right!"

Jess said nothing but walked slowly along, feasting her eyes. After a few moments Kathleen spoke again, in quite a different voice.

"I'm sorry, Jess" she said, "I'm an ungrateful beast. Did you see that little child's face just now when she came running down that slope and saw the flowers? Her expression was just pure wonder. And so should mine be, not just because the daffodils are so beautiful, but because so many people want to come and see them. Thanks for bringing me, Jess."

\*\*\*\*\*

*Lord God, I pray for the gift of wonder, and I ask that I may always treat my fellow men and women with tolerance and respect.*

\*\*\*\*\*

Sometimes I have been for a long walk in the hills and to my delight not met a single person. At other times I have visited a favourite spot in the height of summer and found it taken over by crowds, noisy litter-throwing crowds. I have felt cross and disgruntled and then, catching sight of a happy face, realised that I have no more right than anyone else to enjoyment of the place and that it is good when people are having fun.

The time when I was most tightly hemmed in by a crowd was at Taizé, in France. I was in the great chapel, just one among more than a thousand people. We were all sitting or kneeling on the floor, and bodies pressed against me on every side. There was absolute silence, because everyone was praying. It felt wonderful, then, to be part of a crowd.

# Diana

Diana is eighty-nine. She is afflicted with arthritis, angina and cancer but she does not let any of this trouble her. She lives alone with her brindled cat in an old cottage deep in the country, and she spends her days painting and praying and walking across the hills that surround her home.

Diana seeks God and peace and beauty in that order, and like all hermits who love to dwell in solitude and silence, she gives a warm welcome to all visitors, all strangers who come her way.

The door of her house is never locked. And above that door, in beautiful lettering, the following words are engraved:

Visit we beseech thee O Lord this dwelling place and banish from it all snares of the enemy.

Let thy holy angels abide here to preserve us in peace and may thy blessing be upon us everywhere. Amen.

*****

*Dear Lord, I thank you for Diana. She has no wealth, no power and no wish for either. She is old and ill and an inspiration. May your holy angels guard her always.*

*****

People like Diana are an inspiration. There is so much about old age to sadden us: the diminishing of our mental powers, the increase in our bodily afflictions, the deterioration in our appearance, the loss of value in the eyes of some younger people. It isn't much fun to be labelled a Wrinklie, or, even worse, a Crumblie.

But Diana loves life to the full and enjoys it. No longer beautiful in any conventional sense, she has a grace and gentleness that appeals to everyone who meets her. In her old age she has attained the simplicity and wonder of a child. She gives joy to so many others and is greatly loved.

# Who cares?

Joanna had not been to church for several months. There were two reasons for this. First, she had been angered one Sunday morning when the vicar in his sermon had virulently denounced all homosexuals. Joanna had been particularly upset to think that there might well have been a number of gay people in the congregation and she was thankful that her friend Lyn, a lesbian who had recently set up home with her partner Molly, was not a church-goer.

But Joanna was used to the ideas and opinions of this particular vicar, and although she was often hurt and outraged by some of his pronouncements, her faith in God was strong.

The main reason she had not been attending church was that all her energy was taken up with Rosie, her four-year-old-daughter. She was very ill with cancer and Joanna had just been told that there was no chance of her recovery; she would die within the next few months.

One evening, about a week before Rosie died, Joanna felt more distressed than ever before. She had been advised to leave the hospital for a few hours while Rosie slept. The house was cold and empty. Joanna paced up and down, tears streaming from her face. She could not bring herself to eat or read or watch television.

"I've got to do something" she thought, "I can't go on like this!" Her eye fell on the pile of mail that she hadn't even glanced at for weeks. She picked up a sheet of blue paper and saw that it was a list of talks to be given in her own church during the Autumn. There was one that night, billed as "Spirituality for Women".

"I may as well go" said Joanna to herself. "If I stay here I will go mad."

The talk was a disappointment. It seemed to be simply a history of feminism. But at least it had whiled away two hours and she saw a few familiar faces among the people making for the door. One or two noticed her and smiled or waved. The vicar shook her hand and said it was nice to see her. Then she felt someone touch her shoulder and turned round to see Lyn.

"Lyn! What a surprise!" she exclaimed.

"I know," Lyn said, "I don't normally darken these doors. But when I saw the poster I thought it sounded interesting, so we came along." She smiled ruefully. "It was deadly boring wasn't it?" Then she looked more closely at her friend.

"Hey, Joanna," she said, "you look awful. Whatever's the matter?"

Joanna couldn't stop the tears coursing down her cheeks.

"It's Rosie" she sobbed, "She's dying."

Lyn called to her partner.

"Molly" she said, "come and meet Joanna. We're going over to her house now and we're going to stay with her until she feels better."

"But – " Lesley began.

"No buts, love" said Lyn firmly. She led the way out of the church, her arm round Joanna.

*Dear Lord, keep me from prejudice and a narrow outlook. Help me to look always for the good in others. Give me the sensitivity to realise when those I meet are unhappy or in need, and let my response be generous and sincere.*

Most of us are prejudiced in some way or other, and often we are unaware of it. In our society there is still widespread prejudice against homosexuals and/or black people, to the extent that people can be surprised when a lesbian or a Pakistani is outstandingly brave or kind.

Jesus underlined such prejudice in his story of the Good Samaritan. Jesus was a Jew, speaking to Jews. He knew that most Jews despised Samaritans, and so it was a Samaritan he chose to be the one in his story to show compassion to his neighbour.

It is helpful to look at ourselves, to try to discover where our own prejudices lie. And it is important to realise that those who suffer from the judgemental attitudes of the majority need our understanding and support. Perhaps those of us who are white, heterosexual and able-bodied are especially called to stand up for the rights of the underprivileged and marginalised among us.

# Salomon

When Salomon was about twenty-three years old he came from Belgium to the community where I was living so that he could improve his English. He was a quiet, pleasant lad, slightly built with black hair, brown eyes and finely-boned features. He worked hard in the garden.

One evening, when he had been with us a couple of weeks, Salomon came down to our house with some other young people. After a while, to draw him into the conversation, we asked him to tell us about himself.

His English was very halting, but there was a French girl with us who acted as interpreter, and as Salomon's story unfolded the room became silent, the listeners spellbound.

Here is the gist of what he said:

"Now I live in Belgium. But I was born in the furthest part of Turkey up in the hills away from any towns and between the great rivers, the Tigris and the Euphrates. In our small village everyone was Christian and the language we spoke was Aramaic, the language of Jesus. Nobody except the priest could read or write. We had no clocks or watches, and no-one knew their date of birth. We had no gas or electricity, no radios or television or motorcars.

When I was five years old I was sent to look after the sheep. I was given a gun to keep off the wolves.

This was our life. We never left our village and we had very little idea of what was happening in other parts of the world. Then, suddenly, almost overnight, our world was shattered, turned upside down. Bands of Kurds arrived in our village. They tried to force us to become Muslims.

We refused to do this, all of us. But it meant we had to run away. We left the only place we had known and became refugees. Eventually we were flown to Belgium, and on that journey, in the space of a few hours, we passed through about nine centuries. For my parents especially it was a terrible shock.

Now we live in the civilised world. There are a lot of us Aramaeans living close together in the town of Liège. I see that we are different in many ways from the people of western Europe, but the biggest difference of all is this: what matters most to the Europeans is to have (avoir). What matters most to the Aramaean people is to be (être)."

When Salomon finished speaking we were quiet for a few seconds. Then someone asked him if he would say the Lord's Prayer in Aramaic, just as Jesus said it. We listened, and silently prayed with him.

It was an awesome moment.

*****

*Lord, Salomon's story is a revelation: his was a way of life almost beyond our imagining. Teach us to see ourselves clearly, and to seek simplicity above sophistication. And let us, too, learn to be concerned not so much with having, as with being.*

*****

For me, it is a great joy to spend time with people from other cultures. I rejoice in our differences: kinds of food, ways of dressing, music, emotional responses. Best of all perhaps are the mutual expressions of regard and acceptance, from the graceful "namaste" of an Indian to the four kisses of a Parisian!

But with Salomon there is an extra dimension. He is a foreigner from a very different culture, yes. And he also belongs, at least in my perception, way back in history. His people were uneducated, isolated, cut off from the rest of the world as surely as a remote tribe of South American Indians. Their values were completely different: not only did they have no money, they didn't even know about money. They were not concerned with having and getting, they were untouched by materialism.

Salomon lives in Belgium now. His brothers and sisters and cousins have all adapted well to the western way of life. They are working hard, making money, striving for success. Salomon alone of his generation of Arameans in Belgium, does not work. Although he is only in his twenties, he is looked upon as their leader, because he believes passionately in holding onto the traditions of his people and is doing all he can to preserve their story.

It is easy to fantasize about the good life of these people, living in the back of beyond, untouched by civilisation as we know it. But in reality I know that I would hate it: not being able to read, enjoying none of the comforts of modern living, listening to the howling of the wolves.

And yet I fervently hope, that along with their history, Salomon and his people will be able somehow to hold on to their ungrasping attitude to life.

# Lennie

Lennie is black. He grew up in the slums of a big American city.

Lennie was born to parents who could not cope, with him, with each other, with life. One day when he was eight years old he was sitting on his father's lap when his mother came in with a gun and shot his father dead. She was sentenced to eight years in prison; Lennie was put into Care.

He was unhappy in a succession of foster homes and kept running away. By the time he was ten years old he had become an alcoholic, involved in petty crime and drugs. He became a member of a street gang and violence was his way of life.

When he was seventeen, under the influence of drugs and as part of gang warfare, Lennie killed a man in a rival gang. He was arrested and after trial was sentenced to eighty years in prison. He never saw the solicitor appointed to defend him and was sent down on the testimony of one woman who was not even involved in the case. Lennie has a friend, Judy, who loves him and has faith in him. Because of her, and others of her friends who want to help him, Lennie is not without hope.

Nor is he without courage. The gangs of the kind he was involved in operate in jail, and Lennie had recognition as a strong gang member. Through the influence of Judy he came to realise the evil of his way of life, but he knew that to leave the gangs was very likely to mean his death.

In the event, when Lennie stated that he wanted to leave, he was beaten so badly by other gang members that he very nearly died.

Lennie is twenty-six now. He needs a review of his case. He wants his sentence reduced. He would like to marry Judy. But he is black, a convicted murderer, classed as a no-hoper.

*****

*All-compassionate Father, I pray for Lennie and those like him. I pray for all prisoners, all victims of injustice, and all who are close to despair.*

*****

I am an optimist. I believe in the "spark" of goodness hidden in all men and women. I believe in hope.

But when it comes to Lennie, I find myself faltering. I know enough about American prisons to realise that especially for black prisoners they are horrific. Their notoriety is well attested. Duncan Campbell, the Guardian's Crime correspondent, wrote on 28 February 1995: "Looking to America for penal guidance is like giving an arsonist the keys to an oil tanker."

I can see no way out for Lennie from his deadly situation, no future promise, no freedom until he is an old man, no quality of life, no chance of a fulfilling relationship or a satisfying job.

I know that there are hundreds of others, in situations similar to Lennie's, and I know that organisations which try to help them are frustrated through lack of power and public understanding. But although I have not personally met Lennie, I have met two people who love him, and like them I pray for him regularly, so that his suffering in particular has become real to me and heart-breaking. I am trying to hold on to hope for Lennie, but it feels rather like hanging on from a roof-top by my fingernails.

# Tooth fairy

The young teacher, Rosalind Tempest, was in the middle of telling a story to her class when one of the children cried out "Ouch! Miss Tempest, my tooth's fallen out!"

Rosalind jumped up and went over to the little girl. It was the first tooth she had lost and she was obviously frightened and near to tears. Rosalind lifted her up and sat down with the child on her lap. All the other children were quiet, watching and listening.

"It's all right, Jenny," Rosalind said. "It's a bit of a shock, but don't worry, it happens to everybody." She took the tooth from the little girl and held it up for the children to see.

"Now you must take great care of this tooth, Jenny," she said, "and as soon as you get home you must put it under your pillow. When you wake up in the morning you'll find a nice surprise."

Gemma, one of the more irrepressible infants, was waving her hand wildly. "Miss Tempest!" she called, "I know what happens. The tooth fairy comes! When I woke up next morning, the tooth had gone but there was a pound coin under my pillow!"

"Hey!, that's not fair" said a boy called Garth. "The tooth fairy only left me 20p!"

Everyone looked at Rosalind, waiting for her comment, but before she could think of a convincing explanation for this discrepancy, a sad, adenoidal voice broke the silence,

"I tried to put my tooth under my pillow, Miss," said Darren, "but my Mum saw me and she threw it in the dustbin."

*****

*Lord, we know that in your eyes we are all equal, that you have no favourites. But we, because of our lack of justice have created an unjust society, where many live in poverty and deprivation. Help us to be sensitive to the needs of others and to be willing to work for justice.*

*****

On the face of it this story is about a very trivial incident in an infant classroom. But Darren, in his sad remark, stands for all who belong to the underclass, the poor, the underprivileged, the disadvantaged. Other children received a pound or twenty pence from the tooth fairy, but she didn't even come to look under Darren's pillow because his mother had thrown the tooth away.

Of course we cannot know why she did this. It may have been because she was very poor, it may have been because she was too overburdened with worries of one sort and another to indulge her young son. Perhaps she was insensitive, perhaps she had strong principles about filling young children's heads with fiction or fantasy. We simply do not know, and this itself is a reminder of how we are never qualified to judge people's behaviour, since we do not know the real causes behind what they do.

People are often derided as do-gooders, because they try to understand what it is in a young person's make-up or background that makes him commit criminal acts like mugging or robbery with violence. And yet all of us to an extent behave the way we do because of what has happened to us in the past and the people who have influenced us. There is no question that vicious and violent acts are evil, but there is a question over our attitude to those who perpetrate them. We know very little about Darren: only this single tiny incident in his young life, but it is not difficult to imagine his home life, his upbringing, and the sort of future he might expect.

# Christmas story – 3

Norah was delighted and proud when she was given responsibility for the parish Christmas crib.

It was no ordinary crib, just as St Stephen's was no ordinary church. It was the oldest and biggest church in town, and took up one side of the main square. At Christmas time the crib was placed outside in a prominent position near the main door of the church, where passers-by could easily see it and, Norah fervently hoped, be reminded of the true meaning of Christmas.

She took a lot of trouble over the crib. The figures, more than double life-size, were kept carefully wrapped in tissue from one Christmas to the next, and sometimes Norah touched up the haloes with gold paint. She had knitted a soft white blanket which she tenderly wrapped round the figure of the Christ-child, and every year, early in December, she made a special journey to her brother's farm to collect fresh straw for the large wooden box that represented the manger.

Year in, year out Norah was complimented on the crib and she was very happy with her responsibility until one memorable Christmas Eve.

The vicar, David, was saying his morning prayers when he heard urgent knocking. He opened the door to Norah and to his dismay saw that she was red-faced and wild-eyed and shaking.

"Norah! Whatever's happened? Come in – "

"No, Vicar," said Norah. "Something terrible's happened! I want you to come and see."

David grabbed his coat and scarf and followed Norah out into the raw morning. It was barely light and a few snowflakes were falling. Norah led the way across to the front of the church.

"Look!" she said, pointing at the crib. "It's disgusting! It's an outrage! My crib!"

The figures of Mary and Joseph and the infant Jesus had been thrown onto the ground. David stood still, shocked. But Norah tugged at his sleeve.

"There's worse," she said, "come and see."

David followed her over to the crib and looked inside. A boy, perhaps thirteen or fourteen years old, with a thin white face lay curled up on the straw, Norah's blanket wrapped round his neck. He was fast asleep.

Suddenly Norah's hand shot out. She shook the boy hard, shouting "Get out! Get out! How dare you?!"

The boy opened his eyes, gave a startled look at Norah and David and leapt from the box. He was out of sight in seconds.

Norah began to cry. "How can people be so wicked?" she asked. Then she bent down. "Look, Vicar," she said, "the worst thing of all! The baby, Jesus, is broken!"

*****

*Lord Jesus, give us eyes to see clearly, and a true sense of perspective. Let us not forget that we may find you in the least expected places and people.*

*****

I found this story moving because it presents us with a very human situation, one where no black and white judgements can be made. Who was "good" and who was "bad"? On the face of it, Norah was a good woman doing the best job she could. We can't know whether she did it for the glory of God, or the church, or herself – probably a mix of all three.

Naturally she was angry when she saw what had happened to her crib – so much so that she completely failed to see how appropriate it was for the "home" of Jesus to provide a refuge for someone homeless. Surely the crib was put to far better use as a shelter than as an ornament.

On the face of it the boy was bad, throwing out the image of Jesus, destroying something that was obviously of significance. He may or may not have known about sacrilege; he may not have cared. He may have been drunk or affected by drugs; perhaps he was simply very cold and very tired, and grateful to have found a comparatively warm bed.

I wonder what God thought about all this? My guess is that he would just smile, on both Norah and the boy.

# Frank

Frank is a good man, a committed Christian who follows Christ in the way he lives, serving and loving others.

Frank is an alcoholic who has drunk no alcohol for twenty years. He is one of those people with whom you can relax completely. You don't need to tidy or dust the house when Frank is coming, nor do you have to be anything other than you are, or pretend to be feeling anything you don't feel. He is a real friend.

Frank has been to "the bottom", enduring weeks of utter despair. He once told me how, when he was in this state, another alcoholic, who also happened to be homosexual, came to him every day where he lay in a sort of stupor, and held his hand for hours, just saying over and over again,

"You'll be all right."

Frank said it both sustained him and wore him out, until finally one day he said, "Bugger it, God! You can take over" – which was his way of saying, "Thy will be done." It was a very long haul from there, but now he is happily married and working hard at a steady job. Most of his spare time is spent helping other alcoholics.

*Lord of compassion, I pray for all those who for whatever reason find themselves unable to cope. I pray also for those who are faithful and persistent in giving love and friendship to such people.*

*****

So many people in our society are marginalised: alcoholics like Frank, drug addicts, ethnic minorities, people with AIDS, the disabled, homosexuals, sometimes the old, sometimes women.

Some of these groups are also stigmatised. They are the ones that have to endure a double dose of suffering. To be an alcoholic, or addicted to drugs, to have AIDS, to be disabled is painful and tough, but on top of their desperate struggle to cope such people are too often the victims of prejudice and even cruelty.

Frank was a man of rare courage and generosity. He managed to overcome his addiction and then gave his time and energy to others with the same problem. From being despised and rejected he became respected and admired.

# Daffodils

The Staff nurse was old-fashioned: a sort of stereotype of brisk, no-nonsense efficiency. She was getting me ready for the examination which I knew would be painful.

"Now, Mrs Dove" she said, "there's no need to worry. It will hurt a bit but you just relax and think about what's happening."

"But I don't want to think about it!" I said, dismayed at the very idea.

At that moment the doctor came in. He smiled and said

"What would you like to think about?"

My eyes fell on the vase of daffodils on the window-sill.

"Daffodils" I said.

The doctor was drawing on his gloves.

"Would you like me to recite a poem for you?" he said. I thought almost simultaneously, "What a lovely idea!" and "I hope it's not 'I wandered lonely as a cloud'." But I needn't have worried.

As I listened to the doctor's pleasant voice I forgot all about what he was doing. I didn't even notice the pain.

He knew his Herrick, and began:

Fair daffodils, we weep to see
You haste away so soon;
As yet the early-rising sun
Has not attained his noon.
Stay, stay
Until the hasting day
Has run
But to the evensong;
And, having prayed together, we
Will go with you along.

We have so short time to stay, as you,
We have as short a spring;
As quick a growth to meet decay,
As you, or anything.
We die
As your hours do, and dry
Away
Like to the summer's rain;
Or as the pearls of morning's dew
Ne'er to be found again.

A man of many talents, that doctor!
The poem was especially poignant for me as I was
approaching my fiftieth birthday at the time.
When I thanked him, he grinned and said,
"I suppose I could be struck off for that!"

*****

*Lord, I thank you for beauty, for poetry,*
*for people of humour, tact and generosity.*

*****

For me this was an experience of blessing. I had expected pain and discomfort; instead I was given sensitive consideration, beautiful poetry, thoughts of daffodils and a good laugh.

Unexpected happiness is all the more vivid for being a surprise.

# Lest we forget

In Germany during the Second World War, in every town and city, the Jews were being hunted out and carried off to concentration camps to be murdered.

Naturally the Jews were terrified. In desperation they tried to find hiding places, tried to find people who would help them. But this was almost impossible. Jews had tended to keep to themselves and although many people felt no particular hostility towards them they did not usually regard them as friends. Non-Jews were terrified too; they knew very well what would happen to anyone giving shelter to a Jew.

But in a small town close to the Dutch border, one man overcame his fear. He was a Roman Catholic, and he felt great compassion for the suffering Jews. He took one of them into his home and hid him in a safe place so that when the house was searched he was not discovered.

Eventually the Jew succeeded in escaping and managed to reach a neutral country, but the Catholic man was not so fortunate. He was found trying to help other Jews and was sent to Auschwitz where he was killed.

The Jew is still alive, an old man now, living in Jerusalem. He has planted a tree in memory of the friend who saved him.

*****

*Dear Lord, I ask that I may never forget those who help me when I needed them.*

*I ask that you would plant in me the desire to befriend and support all those who have need of me. Let me never discriminate unfairly between Christian and Jew, Buddhist and agnostic, animist and Muslim. Let me accept all who come my way, as you accept all your children, and let me be ready to learn of you from them.*

*****

Jesus said, "A man can have no greater love than to lay down his life for his friends" (Jn 15:13).

But the man in the story laid down his life for someone who was not originally his friend, someone of a different faith. Love like this is rare: it humbles us and gives us hope for humanity.

Fifty years on from the Second World War, there is a happier, stronger relationship between most Christians and Jews which continues to grow. We are becoming less exclusive, less complacent in our traditions, understanding that the Holy Spirit can never be confined to any particular religion. God is in the place and among the people (of whatever faith or none) where real love is to be found.

# That they may all be one

Helen is not most people's idea of what a minister should be. She must be around thirty, but looks about twenty. She has unruly reddish hair and a puckish sort of face with big innocent eyes. In the garden of her Manse she keeps three black pigs: Grace, Prudence and Joy. Except for official occasions, Helen wears flamboyant colours, buying all her clothes at charity shops. On Sundays, though, and for ecclesial celebrations, she wears a pale blue stock, and thereby hangs this tale.

One Saturday a lad from a family in her parish was to marry a Roman Catholic girl. Helen was asked to take part in the ceremony, so she drove across to the church, dressed in her Sunday best, in time to meet the Catholic priest before the service began.

He welcomed her politely, and beamed when he saw her pale blue stock.

"Ah!" he said approvingly "Our Lady's blue."

"Ah yes," said Helen, looking him gravely in the eye, "but I'm wearing orange knickers!"

*\*\*\*\**

*Lord, plant in us a true desire for Christian unity and grant us the inestimable gift of a sense of humour.*

*\*\*\*\**

Rightly, we are all very serious about the things that matter: politics, justice, education, morality and religion. But sometimes the seriousness can become counter-productive.

I care very much about Christian Unity. I read books and articles on the subject, go to meetings and conferences about it, discuss it day in, day out and try to live it. Sometimes it all seems too much. I am weary of the subject, on the verge of being "burnt out".

Then I hear about Helen and her little joke. I imagine the expression on the Catholic priest's face and I begin to smile.

"How good, how delightful it is", the psalmist exclaims, "for all to live together like brothers." (Ps 133:1)

And how good and delightful it is to share a laugh from time to time.

# Prayer board

Every morning early, after he had opened the church, the first thing Paul the curate did was to go to the porch where the board for prayer requests was fixed to the wall.

He would take it down and carry it to one of the front pews where he would kneel in prayer, spending some minutes on each of the names and requests there.

Sometimes his mind wandered, as he wondered who Harry or Phyllis might be and what their problem was. At other times he was deeply saddened to read "for my son David dying of leukaemia", or "Pat, suffering from serious depression".

One morning in November there was only one request on the prayer board. It was written in the shaky script of an old person:

"I was beaten up at Croydon Bus Station. Pray for them." Pray for *them*? Paul stared at the board, battling with a violent surge of anger. When he felt calmer, he walked to the front of the church and knelt down. For a few moments he prayed fervently for the old man or woman who had been attacked. Then, with some difficulty he began to pray for the assailants. Finally he prayed for himself.

*****

*Lord, help me to have a right and balanced attitude towards violence. Let me show compassion to all victims, and make an effort to understand those who inflict hurt on others. Let me never shy away from the search for true justice.*

*****

There are people who will never make the headlines, never appear in the media at all, unremarkable people. They will not have been particularly noticed as children by their teachers at school and in adult life the spotlight will never shine on them.

Among such people there are saints. Not the sort who will ever be candidates for canonisation, nor demonstrably wonderful people like St Teresa of Avila, St Francis, Ghandi, Mother Teresa or Nelson Mandela. The saints I mean are known as such only to God, or perhaps to the few who live close to them. One of these was the vulnerable old person who took the trouble to go to church to write a petition for prayers for the people who had attacked him or her with violence.

Christians are asked to pray for their enemies; Buddhists meditate on their enemies with loving compassion. This man or woman took a step further in holiness and goodness, by anonymously begging for prayers for those who had hurt him or her.

"Let us now praise famous men" it says in the Book of Ecclesiasticus (44:1).

There are others too who deserve our praise.

# Rosalie and Norman

With several hundred others, I attended a weekend conference on Poverty and Unemployment. We listened to several speakers, all knowledgeable in their subjects: politics, economics, statistics, all genuinely concerned for the underprivileged.

But most of us were especially looking forward to the Sunday morning when we were to hear some of the poor and unemployed speaking for themselves. It was not a disappointment. The testimonies of the four people who told us about their lives were moving and humbling. There was a middle-aged father of six with no hope of finding a job, a single mother struggling to bring up three children, a young man who was the third generation of his family to be long-term unemployed and there was Rosalie.

For some reason, perhaps because she was young and vulnerable and because it obviously cost her a lot to stand up and speak to a large audience of mainly middle-class people, my heart went out to Rosalie.

She was sixteen, small and blonde, wearing a black leather mini-skirt and a sweater several sizes too big for her. Her talk was very short and to the point. She told us that when she became homeless the only place she could find to sleep was a shed full of dustbins, smelly and cold. Friends told her to find lodgings, or a bed and breakfast place. But she was too young. They told her to apply for benefits. But she was too young. She had no home and no money. She lost all her self-confidence and soon became depressed. She finished by saying "I didn't get nothing from nobody."

During the last session of the day people were invited to speak from the floor, either to comment on the weekend or to suggest the kinds of action we might take. Those who wanted to speak raised their hands and a woman with a microphone hurried to them so that everyone could hear. At the very end the chair person indicated someone in a far corner of the room. "I'm afraid that this will have to be the last speaker" she said.

The man stood up. He was not the sort of person you would have noticed in a crowd. He did not tell us his name, but afterwards we learnt it was Norman.

Norman was in his fifties. He stood very still and straight. He spoke with great dignity but all through his speech his mouth was just not trembling and I guess he was hard put to it not to weep.

He told us that he had been made redundant three times. The first time it was bearable, the second time it was awful, the third time it was devastating. He suffered a nervous breakdown, was admitted to a mental hospital and given electric shock therapy.

Not long afterwards, to his great joy, Norman found a job. He was to be responsible for the care of seven old men in a residential care home. He was absolutely delighted and threw all his energy and compassion into the work, studying the individual needs of the men and befriending them.

One day, when he had been five weeks in the job, the Matron called Norman into her office.

"I'm afraid I have bad news for you" she said.

Norman braced himself. "My work's not good enough?" he asked.

"On the contrary" said the Matron, "your work is excellent. We are really impressed with you. But we have only just received your medical report and I see you have been a patient in a mental hospital. I'm afraid you will have to leave."

Norman told us, "It was as though I had been struck with a knife."

Then he said, and for the first time his face relaxed a little, "The Church saved me, the Methodist Church. They have made me Property Steward and at last I feel fulfilled."

*****

*O Lord our God and loving Father, help us not only to care, not only to pray but also to take action on behalf of all those who like Rosalie and Norman, suffer from injustice. Fill our hearts with your generosity, courage, determination and the willingness to share our time, our talents and our money with your sisters and brothers who are in need.*

*****

Poverty and unemployment – these are key issues that concern all of us who want justice in our world. Faced with such enormous problems which are bound up with politics and economics, with greed and with ignorance, we feel powerless.

Many people in Britain are moved by the plight of animals who are treated inhumanely; sadly these same people seem to be less moved by the plight of the homeless, the asylum seekers, the victims of racism, the poor and the unemployed, in other words, by fellow human beings in distress.

Yet without solidarity we can scarcely hope to effect change. Efforts to change the attitude of governments and ordinary people are in the main fruitless. Letters to Members of Parliament, letters and articles in the media, signed petitions all seem to make only minimal impact. It seems impossible to shift the mindset of those who are motivated by greed and a desire for power, or so distant from "the sharp end" that they simply have no idea of how people suffer.

Norman in the story said he was "saved by the Church". Perhaps it is our churches, our Christian communities, who are now the only recourse for those who want to see justice done. Perhaps we should be bombarding our church leaders rather than our politicians with letters and petitions. Perhaps it is up to the people at the grass roots, working ecumenically across all the traditions and with those of other faiths, to take organised, productive action on behalf of the disadvantaged. Those of us who want to be witnesses for Christ can choose to be witnesses for peace and justice in our world.

# Sareth – an epilogue

Sareth is a Cambodian. He had to flee his country as a refugee, and when he managed to return home he had no house for his wife, his six children and himself. Sareth was an amputee. His legs had been blown off when he accidentally trod on a landmine.

Sareth was helped by an aid agency. They found him a house and set him up in business with a few other amputees. Their job is to make basic wheelchairs, using whatever materials are available locally, such as bicycle parts. There is never a shortage of customers, because there are 40,000 Cambodians who have lost limbs in this way, and sadly there will be thousands more as so many landmines remain lethally active. One in every 236 people in Cambodia is an amputee. In addition to his paid work, Sareth gives most of his spare time to help and encourage other landmine victims, some of whom are despairing and resorting to begging on the streets.

One day he was travelling alone in his wheelchair in a distant part of Cambodia when more than a dozen young children ran up and surrounded him. At first Sareth thought that perhaps this was a landmine-free area and the children had never seen a disabled person before. But this was not so. The children had all come up to him to tell him they were sorry he had lost his legs.

It turned out that these children were all orphans, casualties of the war. They wanted very much to be educated, but there was no money to pay for their schooling. However, as they cheerfully told Sareth, they were able to learn a little, because some of the teachers let them look through the windows of the school while lessons were in progress.

*****

*Dear Lord of love and mercy, I praise and thank you for Sareth and all those, your children, my sisters and brothers, who live on the other side of the world and whose lives are so different from mine. I thank you that they, who have known so much bitter suffering, are capable of such tenderness and enthusiasm for knowledge and for life. I thank you because they, who have so little, give me, who have so much, hope in humanity and the future of our world.*

*****

I thought I had finished this book when I learnt of the story of Sareth. I decided to include it as a final meditation because it is a story of hope, of something precious salvaged from disaster.

The background of the story could hardly be darker: Cambodia with its terrible recent history of slaughter and ruin, landmines, the deadly and indiscriminate weapons of destruction. But in the foreground move figures of light: Sareth, giving so much energy to help those who have suffered as he has, and the orphan children who wanted to comfort him, who wanted to learn. Such people are the flowers that bloom in the waste land, such people are the ones who make the struggle for justice and for peace in the world and in all circumstances, well worth while.

# Creed

WE BELIEVE in a community that opens its doors to people who flee war, hunger and poverty in search of a better life.

WE BELIEVE in the power of love, not the power of violence.

WE BELIEVE that we are called to share our lives so as to free each other from poverty, racism, and oppression of all kinds.

WE BELIEVE that the resources of the earth are to be shared among all people – not just the few.

WE BELIEVE in a community that has as a priority a response to those who are denied basic human rights and dignity.

WE REJECT a world where people are denied access to warmth, food, shelter and the right to live in peace.

WE WANT to believe in justice, in goodness and in people.

WE BELIEVE we are called to a life of freedom, of service, of witness, of hope.

WE REJECT the idea that nothing can be done.

WE BELIEVE that a time will come when all people will share in the richness of our world, and that all people will be truly loved and respected.

WE COMMIT OURSELVES in the name of God who
    created the world for us to share, of Christ who
    leads us to freedom, and of the Spirit who calls us
    to action.
TODAY WE COMMIT OURSELVES TO WORK TOGETHER TO
MAKE THIS BELIEF A REALITY.


    Taken from "Stay With Us" a CAFOD Refugee Campaign
worship resource book.